TOWARDS BABINGLEY

Also by Paul Berry:

The Cries of Ashes (Scree, 1979)
Legacies (Scree, 1981)
Earth Musk and Country Dark (Outposts, 1982)
A Bequest of Fire (Outposts, 1985)
Homages and Holiday Snaps (Envoi, 1989)
What Leaves May Know (Hub Editions, 2019)

Social history:

Airfield Heyday (Jim Baldwin, 1989)

TOWARDS
BABINGLEY

Paul Berry

Matador
Unit E2 Airfield Business Park,
Harrison Road, Market Harborough,
Leicestershire. LE16 7UL
Tel: 0116 2792299
Email: books@troubador.co.uk
Web: www.troubador.co.uk/matador
Twitter: @matadorbooks

ISBN 978 1803137 049

British Library Cataloguing in Publication Data.
A catalogue record for this book is available from the British Library.

Printed and bound by CPI Group (UK) Ltd, Croydon, CR0 4YY
Typeset in 10pt Minion Pro by Troubador Publishing Ltd, Leicester, UK

Matador is an imprint of Troubador Publishing Ltd

Cover image: Church of St Felix, Babingley, from Night Marsh Lane, Castle Rising, Norfolk
Front flap images: Little Marsh Lane, Field Dalling, Norfolk

First, foremost, for Tina,
to the memory of Geraldeen,
and a girl from Gosforth

CONTENTS

I fill my arms with thoughts of thee,
And press the common air.

O words are poor receipt for what time hath stole away.

John Clare
(1793–1864)

TOWARDS BABINGLEY

At the dried-up husk and fag-end of a life
this is the place to be: a solitary land of

far off farm sheds, fleeting, unattended,
a ruined church, roof-less, Alleluia-less.

Fields and sky are so empty there is time
and space enow to sort a lifetime's losses:

the mothers, lovers and others, the ones
who passed, all those we let slip away.

The cuckoo who stayed late, well into June,
hidden, chiding, mocking, has flown now

replaced by a crow, hunched in mourning
like an undertaker, seen, all-seeing, sentinel,

directing ritual from the bare upper branch
of an English oak, slow-dying top most down.

Perhaps, had it been done as each occurred
the debt of loss would have been lighter, less,

easier to leave smeared across fields to dry,
blunting barbs, before taking back, less raw,

returning over dry, arid tracks where flints,
sharp, unforgiving, pierce unsuspecting soles.

Now cranesbill, briar and bindweed from a
summer rampage of growing jostle the path

entangling those wanting an easy way back,
hindering progress, encroaching like grief.

CHALK STREAM SUNRISE

Walk in on a day beginning,
as a year eases on its shroud; pass dewed tears
on railings, navigate shoe soaking grass,
to a bridge where late berries flaunt.
Always unseen above, the noisy boys
giving it welly, the fury of afterburners
fading casually under the cathedral of sky,
where old Phoebus waking, rises, needing
all his strength to dismiss and dissolve mist.

Where briars and hips guard and dry teasel
teases, catching like lint thistledown's last hint,
pause, watch as reflections and worlds appear,
slowly, from nothing ever there before.
Small fish are revealed, suddenly startled,
as if silver leaves dropped in water twisted
to flick off the very sun that sought them out.
In darkroom trays of autumn streams develop
those pictures we seldom see or chance to take.

SWIFT DEPARTURE

After weeks of watching
swooping airborne feeding,
aerial dances of distraction
at times almost flirtatious,
now, thorough as any lover
without a word or warning,
they have gone, moved out,
left for places far off, new.

Those who watched remain
abandoned again to empty air,
wondering, trawling memory;
reminded that in each lifetime
moments shared with anything,
anyone, so alive, rarely last,
– those times between whiles
seldom more than months.

GEESE RETURNING

Home from some other cold war place:
    squadrons of Brent and Canada geese
        whose dark formations mark fen skies,
    each delta wing or flight ticking approval
of warmer climes, wash and waterland.

With no dead reckoning or constellations,
    breasting clouds and crossing continents,
        undaunted by Undine's waves and ways,
            not needing radar, Gee free geese
                guided by some force beyond stars
    which decides the precise summer days
a nation's ants aspire to aeronautics.

        As many geese as miles travelled
      violate autumn's airspace,
    slipping in by the thousand, un-noticed
under cover of indifference or dark.

And we, ever poorer and earthbound,
rarely fly skies without flame or fire,
seldom look for beauty among clouds.
We wait on heroes, a new Icarus
to lift bodies, thoughts skyward;
or a game to imitate and remind
while vainly we take time to find
a system that mocks a bird.

(Note – *Gee:* navigational system using radio waves
installed in allied bombers during World War II)

FEBRUARY FILL DYKE

Covering fields, the first and last of winter:
Friday's snow cloth worn threadbare, torn
on sharp furrows, stained by pewtered slush
of weekend meltwater, thawed and refrozen.

The train, sharp in early morning light, cuts,
scores squared landscapes like iced traybakes
in Cambridge's patisserie windows, as we head
over crusted fens where the heavy earth rests.

From a distant field a swan rises and airborne
reccies, flapping slow, low, seeking ice-free
dykes or drains, a thawed and running leam,
anywhere to swim, preen and wet webbed feet

numbed, dried by hard unforgiving soil.
Alighting on glinting water, newly sun melt,
a river system's sentinel stretching, thrashing,
shushing wings to hasten the slouch of winter.

THERE IS A WILLOW

A crawfish tail raises clouds,
dusting a chalk stream's bed,
bustling towards the shade of
a willow set askant the brook:

nettled, meadowsweet gaitered,
riven by lightning decades ago,
leaning where sun's reflections
play across bark-stripped flanks.

A century younger, whip-like you
flailed easy at the fen blow's worst,
basked when lucent rivers slowed
as millstones ceased their turning,

stood proud when seas surged in,
untroubled by roads built alongside.
No Ophelias here yet waters wear
summer garlands of poppy, vetch

and dropped forget-me-not floaters,
sky spots crossing a current's cornea.
While touching on exits, endings,
what of yours; how soon for storms

to tease through thinning canopies
and break those roots now timber's
blanched and strength is sapped?
Your heartwood bared and burned,

dark, light as cork, seen through that
gash where heavens slashed.
Passing we hear in light breezes
your quiet soughing, the creaking

of bare branches, your last limbs,
as though you moan at the pain
from this long-drawn-out dying.
Now, willow, who weeps for you?

THROUGH A ROYAL DEMISE

1.
Setting off for Stratford
to see Ruairi from The Archers
playing the last Plantagenet,
Richard, the car park king,
we begin our soak in history
by a canal, buying brownies
from a pub the boater's used.
We sit on the balance beam
of the bottom gate of lock fifteen,
hearing an urgent breaking free
as cold gallons of Grand Union
escape the close confines of oak
and dark brick where weeds grow.
At Weedon, word arrives by radio:
doctors in remote Scottish castles
express concern, her children gather.
Still raw from times and places
leaving mothers freed to rest at last,
news is heard in silence, sensing,
speculating what concern conceals.

2.
Next morning in the bard's town,
not out of place this day in optician's
windows: framed pictures, dark lace
tastefully draped. A few doors down,
amid Goneril Gifts & Tat, severally,
she looks out, handbagged, small, regal
in plastic, butlered by Bart Simpsons,
manically waving sunlit hours away.
In the distance muffled bells peal,
chimes summoning to their source.
It would be joyous but for the tenor
tolling, drawing tears upon the air,
and the unexpected passing footfall
of townsfolk needing succour of
words spoken in sanctified spaces.
Could any place away from home
be better for pausing, reflecting,
scarce four hundred years or more
and half as many feet from a man
who wrote the ways of monarchs.

3.

After pull-outs, proclamations, posies,
it comes to this: a corner of Norfolk
where air is no longer sliced by rotors
of low-flying mid-morning helicopters
and their twenty-minute turn rounds;
days when a Land Rover Defender'd
Defender of the Faith drove herself
from marshes along an eel-tight road,
and we crossed, slow, and in a glance
an un-gloved hand famed for waving
raised thanks from the steering wheel,
before heads scarved and uncovered
passed in cars heading homeward.
Hers close by, a house of local stone
where a driveway's simple farm gate,
always ever open, is closed shut now.
Still heavy along hedges she passed,
this year's glut of blackberries hang,
their straggling show of mourning
one final taste of an era ended.

September 2022

POSTCARD FROM SOUTHWOLD

Abandoned earthworks of castra
confirm what emperors knew:
there have always been threats
along the Angle's Saxon shore.

Even now tensions living alongside,
if not barbarians, the pre-loved cottage
provinces of the city rich, often empty
in towns choking on sere and yellow.

And the sea itself is not unknown
for attrition: old kingdom capitals
crumble along its wave-gnawed edge,
claimed over centuries by currents.

And while we talk of conflicts, see
in mist, dominating close horizons,
like an abandoned suspicious package,
boxes, a sphere and connecting cables

beyond children making sandcastles;
a constant, coastal éminence grise
as looming Sizewell draws its bow.
Small wonder the North Sea frets.

ALDEBURGH TRIO

Up from the misted shingle strand,
sea kaled, stoned and scalloped,
inland north-west by the Borough

Moot, on an uneven lawn, shaded,
dappled by sun-summered leaves
three good friends are gathered:

men whose love was whispered,
are side by side and a woman,
slightly set back, as if in waiting,

watching for some gap perhaps,
a space to open between them,
to ease in & let her dance begin.

Talk in the town said she composed,
was born with music in her blood so
drawn to one born on St Cecilia's day.

They managed two years alone:
watching over him from behind
before, as expected, his lover

arrived, united then to eternity.
Yet wherever now they play,
whatever melodies still to catch,

this finale is right: harboured here,
anchored together in Suffolk soil,
safe from worlds not always kind.

Cold easterlies rustling inland reeds
alight here and in the trees' canopy
create coast sounds of their own

while beachward beyond new graves,
seas rise as though in standing ovation
to a trio who heard in them their music.

(Note – Aldeburgh parish church is the final resting place
of Benjamin Britten, Peter Pears and Imogen Holst.
The men's gravestones record names, years of birth
and death; hers is inscribed with words from Gustav
Holst's *Hymn to Jesus:* The Heavenly spheres make
music for us All things join in the dance)

A DIFFERENT GARDEN

A winnowing wind brings chickens fussing,
skylarks and the kukukooing of feral doves:
familiar sounds in a different garden heard
where scattered ash of bodybox and brass
dust forgotten debris of wired satin flowers.

Bordering trees hinder departing rising souls
where breezes in new leaves sound like seas.
With quiet, polite digestion and solid chewing
five sheep crop, tearing grass from graves.
The same wind sighs over forgotten names,

resting, marble tells, where no shadows fall.
Old Ackie is resting and Verjerie reunited,
a loving grandma among the parish ancients
and one sad child held safe in Jesus's arms.
Peace, perfect peace, gold-etched into stone

marking out the last heirs to calm and quiet.
Newer generations have less need of hush,
immersed amid richer, frantic dins and rush,
to need any succour such resting places bring,
where silence itself smothers the last remains.

BY STEAM TO CARLISLE

Passing kilns in a cutting's cauldron,
through hard stone hewn by navvy grit,
aromas of breakfast bacon trapped in
dining cars, mix with fumes of steam:
best Welsh, the last from Ffos-y-fran.

Drifts of vapour play, snag on gorse,
and quick to crumple, dissolve, while
exhaust clouds belch to the summit,
bringing volume, mist and smuts
to any mizzle topping Mallerstang.

Beyond secreted shake holes and scars,
busy Batty Moss. Walkers and watchers
wave, survey steam's slow, safe progress
over arches sunk feet deep through mire,
to triumph over danger, disease, deposits.

On the footplate one man sits, leans,
looks out, regulates the exhaust beat,
balances power from the alchemy of
water, fossil forest and driving rods.
His marrer swivels, shovels, sweats.

Premier dining's tables are cleared.
Earpods, travel sweets in Tupperware,
red top rags and playing cards appear;
anything but know the scene outside,
beyond those deep, so comfy seats.

Far north of home, few care for rolling
panoramas passing, easily distracted by
the buffet's beer, to glimpse, descending,
those verdant fields where a river snakes
through that other Eden we cannot reach.

A waking voice enquires if the big bridge
has been crossed, is told it has. No matter.
Time for such solace sherbet lemons bring.
Soon they'll capture all this journey means:
a selfie at the Citadel. Behind them, a train.

(Note – *marrer/marra:* friend, workplace colleague.
Dialect, North East England, Cumbria. DH Lawrence
places it in the Derby/Notts coalfield)

ON BLEA MOOR

Beware unforgiving clouds
stalking here – mists that cloy,
cotton wooling arches, rusting rails –
obscuring, cleaning, clearing the view,
blurring everything we scar you with
even smudging into mapped infinity
the name we would know you by
probably once ending with k?

YOULGREAVE

Banktop Co-Op shines wet and silent
for this brief silence before the hour
when church bells mark the passing
of a never-known-a-summer-like-it.
Far off farm lights sparkle: cheap jewels
in moleskin velvet valley folds where
a single car moves, headlights keeping
early closing dark barely a beam away.

Water ribbons down scars to streams
restless with Sunday, bloated by summer
and all that season's misgivings and rain.
Front room lights come on and spill out
silvering grey, spit and polished roads,
while families gather in parlour huddles.
Tea and television bring compensations
and windows frame rehearsals for winter.

FORBIDDING FIFTY

If, during the time children believed
in magic he had secreted that same faith
sons imbue fathers, he could use it now.
Like a wakeful child lifting one corner
of a bedroom net, or listening at a door
silent, deftly, magically peering to see
one lost love reaching her half century.

Is hair still fair and fine as days when
brushes, tangled nests of strayed locks,
jostled aftershave on pink bed-sit sinks?
Are ice cubes sole preserve of drinks
or dropped, daringly to her secret places?
Is skin still peachy where water melted
or bruised, stretched by children leaving?

But seldom is it ever enough to see.
Lift curtains higher, ease open doors,
break cover, talk and make good the past.
Enquire if her questions ever found answers,
ask how and – dare he – with whose help?
Enquire of once oh so simple happiness,
ingratiate with hopes it returned to stay.

But words should not pass between them.
Children must never overhear the histories
of the safe mothers who seldom venture far;
in hallways, bidding sons *don't miss the last bus*
or imploring daughters *don't go too far too fast*.
They do not care to know of lives and larks
like theirs, just worn by care, tamed by time.

And watchers in curtained limbo cannot see
beyond windows, to reflections trapped there.
No alchemy can free locks seized by years,
with only words, struggling like a lost cause,
to create something as real as in those days.
All that remains: a survivor of plundered times
clutching torn, vague petitions forbidding fifty.

STALKER

Someone new has encroached,
penetrated and established a place
among our circle. We are fewer now.

Uninvited, drawn it seems to age –
its weaknesses, never its wisdom
– making alliance with parents first

now inveigles his way with friends.
Never once formally introduced,
we sensed his attendance, unspoken

beside hospital beds, or in the sudden
ringing of landlines and broken voices
telling he had called again, unbidden.

And now he stalks outside by night,
using our dark, non-sleeping hours
to haunt and make his presence felt.

We fear when, how, and plan hymns,
speculate whether they'll remember us;
what of books when rooms are cleared?

Dawn brings ease as day's eyes open
slow and in new light we plan escapes,
to distant places far away from here

knowing well, as night falls again,
that wherever we hide, on a day
of his choosing, he will seek us out.

RAILWAY CLOSURE

(Inspired by Michael W Foot)

The car no longer lives on the drive,
lording it with caked paint tins, freezers,
in a space where, on a cobwebbed beam,
one last trace remains: an enamel sign
telling *To The Trains,* white on maroon,
arrowing where they pulled or shunted

beyond that junction when retirement
switched tracks and direction travelled
from mainlines regulated, diagrammed
by timetables, with missed connections
and travellers ever glimpsed in passing,
to a slow paced branchline to childhood.

Here his cramped and quiet space grew
each birthday, after restorative impulses
and kit builds shared with grandchildren.
Passing loops, points, sidings extended,
felted fields and village streets expanded,
resin residents glued to worlds he made.

Now cleared away, boxed and labelled:
stations, tinplate crossing gates, tracks,
curved, straight, rusting, then treasure –
a plastic box brimming like Woodham's
Barry yard, consigned with black felt tip
in a teacher's plain hand: *locos for repair.*

I see him, leaning in to reach a station,
flicking soft brushes across platforms,
toppling tired commuters waiting there,
bending to nudge stubborn saddle tanks,
reverently rerailing a last proud Duchess
with the easy precision of a steam crane

in this swept, functional, muddled dark
where life for those left still runs to time.
As his image fades on air and gentle dust
some vague aura stays, a presence again.
And the hidden gap amidst the everyday
opens as lives and trains are tidied away.

HE ARRIVED IN AN OXO TIN

with a lid pierced through with holes.
A small ball of fur, far from home,
faintly redolent of damp sawdust,
shrouded in shredded paper as if
aping a premium packaged gift.
For his living soul mere shillings,
yet pounds for the metal cage.
Uncurling each evening
to a country not his own,
stoic, making the best of it,
twitching whiskers, preening,
cleaning, tidying the space.
Always cute hunkered up,
paws pouching peanuts for
hiding in the larder store.
Sometimes for a good run
given freedom of the room;
floor tiles, carpets they said,
on the flat within four walls
with no venturing off-limits.
Defiantly he would emerge,
slow in his own sweet time,
too long in theirs, from deep
in the sofa's dark, triumphant
along a frantic trail of cheese.
Good to be adventurous, free,
when lives are so long caged.

All night their squeaking treadmills
are descant for the sleeping hours
and golden hamsters in solitary again
are hanging from their prison bars.

TO 36, A CALF

Regret or a beast's dead weight
dogs his heavy footfall uphill,
hoi hoi-ing the herd dairywards.
Across his back and shoulders
a calf straddles, lolls head down,
red tongue protruding, drooling.
In a stone wall's lea, manic crows
cavort upon protein-slimed grass,
marking where a birth has been.

Alone, number 36 wanders fields
while others crop contours below,
resting, cudding in the evening sun,
their yeilds met, a day's work done.
And she, with withered bag hanging
like a second bloodied tail and still
sweet with her offspring's smell,
cries from the heart, hoarse, throaty,
but no answer from unforgiving hills.

Sky-high through silences planes move;
those in flight between cities, unaware
of small tragedies in the fields below.
By sunset she returns to lower fields
searching, third time in as many hours,
rending valleys with unanswered cries.
Roused, 54 and 28 nudge their heads
into hers, provide a flank to lean on,
offer the love mothers are wont to do.

HARVEST THANKSGIVING

In a time of woodsmoke and burning leaves
memories smoulder of a school harvest home;
of the baker's glazed and caught bread stook,
large and leaning, at altars of chancels cauli'd
and carrotted. And in the nave we serried poor:
knaves, rascals and urchins from families who
toiled to grow, who knew the snow in winter,
needing sun and warmth to swell the grain.

Later, richer, we turned soil with sons: tilling,
tending, growing proud tubers, beans and beet.
Then to church one autumn Sunday, to mark a
simple faith in the God of earth and nature table.
Eyes drawn to tins, the wilting parish cabbage,
then across fields to chemical and plastic plants
where congregations held management roles,
or shares; and thus directed gave our thanks.

Now coasters load grain at dockside quays,
lost among swirling dust of summers passed,
lorried in from marsh fields, barn and dryer.
Decades on, harvesting supermarket shelves,
hands are uncalloused, clean; gardens grassed.
Lives no longer turn with the season's wheel.
Severed roots wither and there is little need
for harvest home amid a haste to ship it out.

LONGHOLM 2019

Fair dues creating
a 'pop-up' studio
for two in a shed
with arrangements
of retired, rusted
blades, chisels, saws.

Did this lifetimes ago:
paper, brushes
in jam-jar water,
school library hush,
cursing paint cakes,
the inability to draw.

Silence flows easy
broken by whispers,
heaven knows why –
sheds seem to demand
sibilants no louder than
bristles across Bockingford.

(Note – *Bockingford*: high-quality artist's watercolour
paper incorporating woollen felts to create texture)

HAIKU AT LONGHOLM

growing potatoes watch
metal farm trailer
swallowed by fields

summer solstice fenblow
three tight rosebuds
awaiting arrival

iron gate set in hedge
leaves grass sunshine trapped
held behind bars

spade in soil
handle weathered
worn as gardener's hand

beech
bonfire burned
unintentional charcoal

bonfire blackened twig
the charred smell
of scribbled words

sun shadows evening
distant Chinook slices air
wind teasing leaves sssshhhh

STATES

A night with stars and friends,
seldom enjoyed during curfew.
Inside: conversation, candles,
unfunctional food, fancy even.
There were many such nights
in memory, curtailed only by
the first small invading force.

We stocked larders with beans,
ketchups, seldom ventured out
by night alone, hung on, survived
until this short ceasefire when still
in the pause and shuttle of talk
we strain to hear a breath, or faint
boy's voice whose tape has stopped.

Ten times round the sun and back:
we have forgotten rights and freedoms
surrendered when, as speeding Panzers
from some grainy, handed-down war,
prams and bounty boxes swept in,
annexing free spirits to parenthood,
our Abyssinia, Poland and Elysium.

FIXING, THEN & NOW

Scooped hands offer up bright pieces,
a child's voice implores *fisk it daddy*.
There was pleasing faith in those days,
a confidence in things being mended,
lost toys rescued, all restored to rights,
and I, allied to that trinity where only
ignorance, brute force and strong glue
prevailed, most often rose to challenges,
creating and compounding reputations.

Years later he sees through the old lie;
knows while love is endless and endures,
the illusions of security are frail, limited
and finite, whose thin glass shatters now.
These days he arrives with broken worlds,
whole nations in need of healing while I,
knowing no words or ways to repair, renew,
fall back on spring, skybird song, blossom,
the balm of blue in woods worn by time.

BLACKBERRIES

Does he still remember blackberrying here?
The ride out, swerving along rutted tracks
on a bike made to shake every young bone,
his determination to push, pump pedals round,
visible, wending his way to who knew where.

Or first sight of hedges and briars bent heavy?
Fruits swollen, rinsed by rain, dried by breezes,
hold-tight fingers tugging at reds or squashing
berries that barely bled in the gatherer's box
though hands were stained and clotted by pulp.

Or know again the eager return to give his gift?
Proud, as if harvests were from his own planting,
he who had dared the hidden thorns and barbs,
endured pin-pricking pain probing for the best,
for the women in his life then to sweeten or stew.

Does he recall who rode and gathered with him,
who returns decades on to taste and remember
the shared, simple pleasures of a single summer?
Early morning sun casts his shadow upon hedges,
time shifts and at the whim of clouds, he is gone.

HER PICTURE WILL COME DOWN

In a room for pausing, passing through
a girl just happening to be there
smiles with summer in her eyes
& two worlds narrow, converge.

Unseen, unheard, love spills over lives,
swelling until they are smothered,
wading through, thigh high & happy,
slow like syrup, knowing it is new,

sweet & sticky this first & only time,
too perfect and unaccustomed to obstacles.
Years stack beyond unforeseen
endings and her picture will come down

as unexpected as when she first appeared:
the smile worn, those lips another's now,
once fine blonde hair silvering to grey,
face shaped by cares unimagined then.

Now both older, wiser, wider, he looks
through lenses age, wear & tears will blur,
into unforgotten eyes, finding no trace
of summers past, only brooding winter there.

ON LICKBARROW HILL

I would come to you now,
still needing to link our water worlds,
mine of fen & sedge, yours of mere & tarn,
discovering by Lickbarrow Hill a traveller's bench
where you sat those three evenings, captivated,
held by views over rooftops & a calm lake's waves
lapping idly on its western pine tree'd shore.

You, coy girl of science and scripture
parka'd, perched, pretty, eyes searching, always;
becoming aware distance is more than mere miles,
uncertain destinations are for working towards,
together, before long letters in short night hours,
sharing those scenes & triggered longings,
in language worthy of those hill place poets.

Understanding only words in plain order,
& knowing no road to reach you, I stayed rooted.
Near half a century since you & those counties
changed names, now I would come to you,
as dusty envelopes spill their phrases, releasing
biro'd paper's passion, your memories of lakes
amid these wetlands, uniting mists, damp & tears.

ONCE, LIKE A LARK

Once, winter was a season &
he marked its flitting, fired, flung
like a lark into new washed skies,
eager to claim a right to clouds

until one year reaching higher,
soaring above some distant place
circling, saw a small room below:
faded carpet worn and warm,

walls poster plastered & timetabled,
pictures from home, heating rings,
a baked bean pan, butter cooler,
her one bed covered like an altar

where rituals, devotions would begin,
hesitant at first, tentative, coy,
an uncertain skimming of lip with lip
& the slow unbuttoning of spring.

Then winter becomes a destination:
he who dared night now fears the dark,
still the hero he would have been
yet his knowledge of currents forgotten,

no longer reaching keen to swoop, sing
or climb to clouds, bruised & dying now,
to honour rooms & hearts it began in,
those haunting shrines, the relics of love.

TOADFLAX & BIRDSONG

During our time together,
city-girl, I knew the streets
around rooms you lived in
better than my own,

& thought it okay to be so
until you left one city
for another and in our
stepping back, returned

home to sky, field & lane;
needing help naming yellow
that grew in places I knew,
realising that grafting on

or uprooting into new soil
sometimes fails & wondering
if you transplanted here,
hearing a darting wren

or dunnocks fussing over
banks topped with pale
flecks like scrambled egg,
could name the flower

or understand how birdsong
has power to transport,
drawing us back to thrive
close by ancestral hearth-sides.

EASTER COMMMUNION 2020

remembering Geraldeen

Early to avoid compliance men,
I spend my government dole
of exercise, means tested by age,
searching the water-land's edge

for reassuring skies of emptiness
above soil that was a silted sea-bed,
where resident skylarks, startled,
rise to storm the heavens with song.

Hawthorn blossom faintly sweetens
the fetid breath of fertiliser'd fields;
Spanish bluebells and mayflower
brighten the lane to Night Marsh.

Along the sluice a solitary swan
preens, yellowed neck twisting to
arrange and layer each white quill,
like girls among folds of ivory, snow,

and shy with alabaster necks and ears,
brushing, combing out-of-place hairs,
preening fussily for the Whit Walks,
proud parades and first communions.

Tho' white abounds Whitsun must wait
beyond today's Resurrection Sunday
and in this place where, once, water was
we know about returning, transformed.

Tracks are dry, unyielding, whether
shouldering a cross or just a chip;
tractor tyres have crimped the edge
of baked, pastried earth and verge.

Latterly, between plagues, all roads
were like this: dusty, a tumbril wide,
hard trod between villages, hamlets
and bakers selling their daily bread or

give us this day sunlight silvering
dew on pastures where furloughed horses
graze, idle, awaiting ladies of the lord
of a manor for Monday's tacking up.

Returning, a light benediction of rain
softens surfaces; legs, soles ache less
and at the end of seven solitary miles
some other soul might feel blessed.

AT A GRAVE ON CHRISTMAS EVE

Christmas Eve at the cemetery: cars litter verges
already muddied, mulched by autumn's leavings.
Mantels, trees are garlanded; light emitting diodes
challenge darkness eight flickering, twinkly ways.
So now the town turns out, wrapped and wreathed,
to remember the dead and decorate their graves.

I stand empty-handed, wet-shoed among long grass,
bowed, held by those sweet names chiselled in gold,
whose trained fingers once traced the marble's braille,
of the father I feel I know, whom you rest with now.
The untimely tally of your years in gilt screams out
that life had no right to walk out on you when it did.

Maybe the season, our tendency to call unexpectedly,
brings me here, wondering if a previous lover visits,
and how times and passions you told of, changed.
At our last Christmas you gifted a glass, crystal cut,
and Napoleon brandy in a bottle that stayed half full,
as though our days and ways stalled or ended then.

Beside a gate, a standpipe with crumpled milk bottles
where bins, in mourning black, spill dead chrysanths,
their varied stages of decay befitting time and place.
Later, twisting open a bottle's cap of love and memory,
I nose heady scents, buff my glass, restore them back:
how can I drink to health, snatched from you so young?

COLIN'S SUMMER HOUSE

Before you can notice change you must
know and honour how you are now.
PD Ouspensky 1878–1947
(Note pinned inside)

Among the shrubs, his writing place:
a shelter from summer showers
with sturdy chair and bureau desk.
On three sides fading orange
Penguins guard and mock,
while from her paperback spine
Iris Murdoch watches, unsmiling,
at my efforts to mark the page.
Old bottles from Spalding –
long lacking fizz if not their marbles
– interrupt the lines of books.
Last year's leaf-fall eddies
crisp and dry at the door,
high-flyers caught twitching
in the window's crocheted webs.
Outside a fine rain feels new leaves;
the single blackbird sings his space.
Here in my borrowed territory
I can find no song or words,
as the minutiae of another's place
highlights places travelled through,
all those ones passed we failed to see.

SPRING SOWING

Every year the same aches:
muscles tight, palms blistered
and grit darkening finger nails.
I know and recognise the signs,
the sweat and smell of bending.
I know and accept the price
of breaking earth's resistance
after the rest of fallow days,
breaking soil again for growing.

Harder each year with pen, paper
to urge unwilling poems be,
when brute force and salt dew
cannot raise words and ideas
buried like heavy stones below.
Against torpor and a pen stilled
by cold, crusted challenges of pages
I would choose the ache of a spade
slicing earth nearer new beginnings.

VIEWPOINT

Sorry if by
standing in
the middle
of the poem
I
am in the way.
Just try and see
through me.

JOHN CLARE AGAIN

Tweed jacketed, perched on a desk,
legs swinging below like pendulums
helping regulate the enthusiasm
consuming him as he spoke of
a peasant poet's life, work and loves,
the *I Am*-bits and final, asylum years.
An open, worn volume in his hands
but no need to quote or refer to it,
mind and body totally consumed
by another's presence: it was his gift
offered to us, wrapped with passion,
visions of a countryman, long dead.

Across years I bought the poetry, dipped,
played LPs, Britten giving words wings.
Random visits were made: to Stamford
where he walked one closed-down day,
clutching money saved to buy a book,
then returning across fields, a day lost,
empty-handed, empty-bellied, wiser.
In the county town, retraced a route
from asylum to a church portico
to sit out the day or watch passing lives,
reassured his wife raised the children,
but seeing his first love, first and last.

It is a day near the edge of his fen,
a house and garden beside a river
where carriers sailed barges
which once he took to look for work.
A poet and professor's daughter
tells how a father found poems
by a pastoral poet, discarded,
forgotten in a curator's cupboard,
recounting stories of rescuing,
transcribing faded, scribbled papers.
Moments from memory, fuse;
the book a teacher held was his.

The teacher, unwitting voyeur perhaps,
but enthusiasm real and mission true.
For her passion is genuine, familial.
She recalls a father's discoveries,
his scholarly stewardship sharing,
a peasant's view with wider worlds.
Her voice quiet, reverent, as if kin
to a labourer's journeyman son;
linking words, lives and years removed.
Breezes stir leaves, flies fuss, annoy.
In hedge-less fields ripe corn sways.
With us on the terrace, John Clare again.

DRIVING MISS DAISY

(for Mollie)

At 3pm the poetry lady invites us
to do a Frank O'Hara, walk forth
and find the city in her village.
Miss Daisy bids me push her chair.
Reversing the steep herringbone drive
we jostle neighbour John and Poppy,
walking on a lead since the day
of her curiosity on the viaduct.
We part with pleasantries, Poppy
with three legs and Miss Daisy
with four wheels and me.
                              She
spent her wartime here, a child
sent to willing relatives, asking
now to see the pond in splendour.
Signs on garden walls are passed:
We no longer operate the book stall;
Please do not park as access needed;
and now sumer is icumen in,
Due to ill health we will no longer
hold the fete in our garden.
Two blackbirds seem bothered.

We
find her pond in the wrong place
and nod to the nesting parish goose
famed for phantom pregnancies.
Nine others graze Top Common
gingerly swaying over coarse grass,
walking like they have bunions.
One, alabaster white, motionless,
not a feather out of place, as if
made of resin for collectors and
boxed by Border Arts.
We reverse
again uphill through ruts to the manor,
where the child was never allowed to go.
She was, she says, too young, though
why when unfenced water was okay?
Then: look at that poor dead one. What?
That tree. One, only one, leans leafless
by the crab catcher's place whose
plastic boxes are stacked on the green,
safer here than out of sight on an
open beach with his pots and boat.
With no
sidewalks, highways swell with walkers.
Some, like us with pens and pad,
have poems to collect. Others, with
dogs and discreet bags, scoop crap.
We find little of the city though
two dark-brick viaducts whose eight
skewed arches bring railways to the sea,
high over echoes and undulations, seem
better suited to terrace and tall chimney
than flint and verdant green.

                    I was here
long before your number came up,
Miss Daisy boasts as we turn back
for cake and sharing things we've seen.
Yet any advantage hardly matters:
lost rows of cottages, intrusive newbuilds
have warped her memories, creating for us
a level playing field, not there then.
Deep she breathes on lilac-scented air.
Despite a gap in years or legs that work
this much at least, we share.

THE VOYAGES OF UNCLE JOE

Possessing a special brightness
they called Uncle Joe, Sonny.
He knew much of many things
and saw in problems, solutions.
Careful with words, each one
measured exactly to fill the gap,
chosen with care, joining precisely
like the pipes he repaired each day.
No discord or malice ever blocked
and sentiment flowed as it should.
For long years he stifled yearnings
to travel, learn, view civilisations
and see the world's Seven Wonders.
But life took root in Seven Kings.

Hearing hooters of tugs and ships
nudging round Coldharbour's curve
during the Royal Docks' dying days,
his head would turn to listen, smile,
ponder and renew again the plan.
Together, Joe and daughter would
down to the docks, bagsy any ship
and stow away to who cared where.
The Commercial Road was closest
he came, driving the company van
with tools, a dining room chair
and cushions for nipper in the back.
Then each year an Isle of Wight ferry
and holidays over the sea to Vectis.

In cults of music and stereo sound
he was almost a minister, ordained
into repetitive rituals that suited him:
finger-tipped offerings of black vinyl
at the shrine of Bang and Olufsen,
circling surfaces with Emitex cloth
reverent as any church celebrant
with linen cleaning a chalice rim.
Speakers positioned like altar boys
for the best *Reader's Digest* could offer:
the Arcadians, Slavonic dances, Planets,
Hebrides, the halls of mountain kings.
With Mantovani and his Charmaine,
who knew the shores they sailed?

Then, when his brain grew old, rusted,
memories would leak, audibly dripping,
overflowing with troop ships returning.
Engineers who supported desert armies,
a cramped, slow-cooked seaborne stew
of bodies, sweat, salt air and longing,
rounding the Cape and, starboard, there:
Table Mountain with its cloth of cloud.
And so that blighted seed was sown.
Today in some other faraway place,
with ear to the clouds, he hears distant
echoes rising over Rainham marshes:
the deep bass calling of forgotten ships.
    One day Little Nip. One day.

FAREWELL FOREST GATE

A spring day stained by mourning:
limousined, pale sorrowed faces stare
through tears, polished glass and us
to stalls spilling okra and oranges,
the halal butchers where sunsets
of mutton and mixed meats hang,
to swathed rainbows in a sari shop
and Asian jeweller's gold chain falls.

This son of a forgotten empire who
stayed, settled, now slowly departs
for one last time, boxed and labelled.
Flowers the sole concession to colour:
neighbourly bunches, a spray from all
at the eel and pie, lilies of kith and kin.
Thus Terry, Uncle: invested, wreathed,
capital cockney for death's procession,

topped out, spelt in white chrysanthemums
trades one, once strange, place for another.

FELIX AT BABINGLEY

A redundant road that led coastward once,
bridging a river that bends to ruins beyond:
the scene presents itself, as though unchanged.
But there are layers here; dig down, scrape back
time's palimpsest, from defences of fading wars,
through Doomsday's *Babinghelea* and beyond
to Bede who knew and wrote about this place,
of times as distant from him, as he from today.

And of a Burgundian, a priest perhaps, sailing
from the Empire of the Franks, arriving here;
landfall by a settlement where lazy smoke drifts,
whose fetid Saxon scents sting eyes and startle.
Here by invitation of tribal royals, to civilise
and cheer those scrimping at an estuarine edge,
then covering the Angle's land until a kingdom
is crossed and tribes turn, kneeling to the east.

To him is raised a first, crude, fleeting church,
centuries later reaffirmed with brick and stone;
rootless now, ivied in decay, abandoned, empty
yet lording the landscape still, drawing the eye.
A walker passing pauses, taking in the scene,
beguiled by that peace and enfolding stillness,
not the mere air of stale centuries, but a place
offering foothold for something enduring still.

Beyond history's levels, layers and every myth
and legend we have made, it is as if one story
reaches to connect and induce a melting mood.
In fields beside remains, sheep graze coarse grass,
fold at the knee to gain grounded, sweeter stems.
Perhaps a trick they learned way back, bowing
as though to venerate a missioner landing here,
the apprentice saint setting out on his career.

SIMPLY BECAUSE

Simply because she was beautiful he was beguiled:
those first fumbled ecstasies, the cool velvet arbours,
a coy fascination with places suddenly damp.

Simpler secrets were easily missed: ambitions, fears,
deep in harder to discover places, those questions,
future hopes, plans, songs he would never sing.

Simply in ways they could not stop, miles, years,
the heirs of others, divided them. She, in some distant place,
hardly knows or cares how many anniversaries have passed.

Simply because once there seemed so much and now, only this.

TRAVELLING

Once journeys had beginnings:
outward with fond farewells,
returning to eager welcomes.
Today too long, too frequent,
the same unvarying roads
always bypassing towns,
avoiding fond remembered
hamlets straddling the way.
Miles and years have stacked
since journeys made together.
Familiar roads are declassified:
potholes, verge and hedge stray,
encroach as lanes become lanes.
Diversions on dual carriageways
and what-a-relief roads ignored
to favour slow village chicanes.
Sly reworkings reroute traffic,
block ends of the same streets
old lovers left long ago, now
cul de sacs and sad dead ends.
These days no-one is waiting
at home to meet and make
a welcome back, with new milk,
a tin of buns or sorted piles of post.
Journeys are mere picaresques
seldom sealed with endings.

LANDSCAPE HISTORY

Over burgers at a Wimpy in Derby
she disputes that her eyes are sad,
coyly suggesting he leans across,
looks into them, tells what he sees.
He gazes, gladly: *contact lenses.*

In a lane leading toward Licswm
she plucks ryegrass from the bank,
pensively fingering, checking off
tinkers, tailors, soldiers, spies,
the rich, poor, everyone but him.

Poised by a quarry at Rhes-y-cae
he fusses, takes pictures as sun sets,
her hair gold against the ochred west;
speed, focal length, aperture set exact
for Boots to turn the memories black.

She sits on a breakwater at Cromer
in the drizzle of waves crashing in,
aware of smooth pebbles that drop
and how he probably has little idea
what to bring and lay at her feet.

High midday sun warms the Broads:
her borrowed canoe's mooring rope
is frayed, weeded, worn, too wet
to grip or pull the boat toward him
and defy the tides to hold her fast.

On railway bridges crossing the Tyne
a homeward train slows and she looks
down to the quays, chares and steps
once walked and climbed together,
amazed he was ever there at all.

Love seldom ends as beautifully
as it begins. Loping through love,
moments shared snag on landscapes
like wool on barbed fences, lasting
long after the lovers ceased to be.

DAY TRIP WITH MARIE

All I have is this:
a small two by three
by Boots in B and W
of a cousin I barely knew.
Our paddling paused,
she stands beside me,
chunky in her costume,
well fed for the fifties.
My awkward arms
do not embrace
the stranger from London
come on holiday,
whose mum was
an aunt and seldom seen.
Happy to sidle up close,
she shows a hint of smile,
some would say contentment.
Blown by summer wind,
hair has left her forehead,
much as it will at 30
when the tumour takes her.

COUNTRY CHURCHYARD

You were the last to give your lives
to these fields, flints and hearth-sides.
Since your names inked family Bibles
your children have read other books,
stayed at their desk through fruitings,
harvests, pedalled beyond the parish
to far-flung schools for older heads.

You saw market buses weave lanes,
hinting of different delights in towns
no longer a day's brisk march away.
You smelled pre-packed bakehouse air
as yeasty city bread arrived in the shop,
wax papered with printed sunshine,
floured by grains from no fields near.

You have seen known worlds shrink
with timetables and vapour trains,
heard sons talk of hopes, ambition,
something they called expectations,
popular where the grandchildren live.
You visited and ached for a return
to blazing grates or a frozen well.

Seventy summers on: roll call, noticing
names who were girls, boys, mad-wags
from cottage, farm and distant hamlet.
No longer pounding hard playgrounds,
knee-grazed, stone-stiff in churchyards.
All present, correct and neat in line:
roll-called for a final rearguard action.

Run now, flail arms as you did at harvest,
flush out rats and rabbits with your din.
Scream down fields by Whistling Tree,
ruffle feathers of the few fussing hens,
wake the Jolly Farmers, long in repose.
You, who were the last to stay 'til death,
rise up, roam and haunt the village still.

ON SEEING *THE BLIND GIRL*

(a painting by John Everett Millais, 1856)

The dark skies lighten, showers pass.
A girl and her sister unwrap emerge
slow from their hasty blanket shelter,
hands tight gripped against the warming light.
Crude capitals on a chest pinned paper says blind
and her half closed eyes and upward tilted head
confirms a fear moving forward or looking down.
The young sister pulls the coarse cloth
over her own eyes, wonders is this what it's like.
On the unseen torn serge of her lap
an old squeeze-box rests, redundant
when the sympathetic sighted took shelter.
No-one passes with coins to throw for tunes.
Yet there are compensations:
a butterfly lands on her shoulder,
speedwell brushes her hand.
The sun will dry worn clothes and covers,
gilding her never seen auburn hair
and people with ha'pennies will pass again.
Beyond freshened fields, a rainbow is forming
with who knows what at its end,
if only she could see it.

RITES OF SPRING

From far-off marsh field clamps
come muffled morning drum rolls
of the beets dropping into bulkers,
heralding the white-before-green
hedged drifts of blackthorn blossom,
whose sweet nectar faintly talcums
dusky air and spring's new skin.

Twig tip buds split, shy petals hide;
in reeds by March muddied banks
frogs in clinging abandon make love,
grinning satisfaction from ear to ear.
And we, of such age and disposition,
seizing moments of a year's beginning,
shuffling towards our allotted span,

pause to noticeably notice, take in,
and remember it was not always so.
One year a season arrived unheeded
over shires new laid with vernal baize.
Spring was a time for passing through,
in coaches sealed off from landscapes
and roads lined with viridescent may,

headlong to shrines in distant towns
hiding girls with bewitching smiles,
fine hair spun of sunbeams and eyes
perplexed and blue from wondering.
And we, heady with love's blind force
and its first time sap, rooted too deep
in our own greening to notice another.

A MEMORY UNBIDDEN

How do they act, the one-time lovers,
when a memory suddenly surfaces, unbidden,
when names once whispered emerge to shake tidy lives,

or letters are found from long separated nights,
photos in forgotten formats, a scene that held them once,
sparking, arcing speculation about some once familiar he or she?

Startled thus, do they rejoice in recollection,
wondering of their one-time worshippers, knowing now
& reassured that history's precious intimacy was not misplaced;

pause to ponder, frame the wonder with *perhaps...*
perhaps *what if...* if caught off guard, daring to speculate
how, with some other alchemy, years & lives may have differed?

Or react too hastily, pushing pleasures or pain away,
blinding mind's eyes, dulling ears to echoes, stifling curiosity
for fear, submerged, they drown 'neath the weight of remembering?

ROMAN WALL RETURN

Of all those times, places and spaces shared,
it was cool April, leaving city chares and lonnens
for the heart of that goitred northern neck
where stones, hewn and lugged by legionaries,
defended and marked the edge of empires.

In the footsteps of impressed men he came
newly arrived from southern warmer climes,
easily impressed by landscapes and a native girl
luring, leading him, wall walking between forts.
At Highshields resting in the rock ribbon's lee,

gazing beyond Crag Lough and pine-clad hills
where impatient nations replaced painted tribes,
whose screams taunted night's frozen sentinels,
curdling fear in guts of those who guarded here.
Warmed by nearness of each other, lovers lay

revealing hidden secrets beneath thin layers
openly, excitingly daring, skin caressed by breezes,
sung to by skylarks, sharing a picnic her mother made.
South by a Roman mile, eagles ruled and men search,
scraping centuries of earth down to toga'd times

revealing shoes, letters, beads, brushes, invitations:
displays turn ancient domesticity to intimate encounters.
One day he will return, a freed man and alone,
searching for first, wary passions practised here,
hoped to last lifetimes, lost without trace.

Yet there are no museums or shrines for love.
Nothing save a memory of laying among fresh grass,
and her childlike joy when it sprang back on rising, after.
Wisps, threads spun on air, like tunes on border pipes
echoing from moor and sky, teasing him still.

(Note – *chares:* narrow streets, often medieval; *lonnens:* twisting alleys.
Dialect, North East England, particularly hinterlands of the River Tyne.)

LOCKDOWN

Passing the house you left
I search empty windows
needing to confirm, still,
you have really gone.
Daffodils grow below
and hyacinths from all
those Mother's Days
show through on cue.

Stonking 'tutionals the boys
called the walks we shared.
Yet they were always more
than short escapes from home,
diversions from growing old.
A brief reprieve from solitude
when he, of love everlasting,
unknowing, began to forget.

You would lean hard on my arm
and close huddled like lovers,
would dally or wander slow
the clifftop paths and lanes.
Shy violets and primrose clumps
or sunlight sweeping distant skies
shadowing St Botolph's stump
delighted the country girl in you.

As you began to bend, closing
like a daisy on the evening lawn,
this view of neat borders, paths
across a green, became your world.
Cornered on your perching stool,
you would lift the nets, waving,
watching us long out of sight,
before your veil came down.

Now staying home, saving lives,
I feel what lockdown brings;
understanding your eagerness
to force tired limbs, be able
to smile upon simple things
and see places beyond windows
where without thought or cares,
so easily once, we went.

LANES IN A LIFE

(In memory of Mum)

I Beginnings, endings

As you edged nearer dying, often
we walked this lane, nearest in miles,
close by and only one word different
to your childtime's nurturing place,
thinking as endings near, beginnings
need remembering, helping balance
and weigh the worth of years between.
All lanes to nowhere reveal secrets
to any who look or have time to pry,
the trees overhang, bowing to those
who love them, the way of these ways.
Yet none have Prince, the pony, at a gate
with, upshafted, your father's trap waiting
for trips to Thursford meeting the train,
returning safe home the tired and weary
who dared venture to worlds and places
seldom as they seem, or ought have been,
those who should never have left at all.

Always easy with horses, even those
from the Hall, prone to skittish urges
and untroubled by class or bloodline
(it was only you who were), pausing
in your passing, to talk head to head,
returning to your pony's field again,
remembering, regaling, reworking this
puzzling present with the benison of then.

Once, trees scattered wild cherries
along our track and deftly you squashed
none along the bubbled sanded carpet,
dowager heir to fields and country airs.
The lane splits, divides, deeper toward
rural idylls or redundant, cracked old roads.
Instinctively you turn west, marshward,
preferring childhood's unmade wildways
over metalled highways, however agéd.
And I walk here now, more even than

then with you, as years invisibly mount
in the space since your passing. Yet
time's numbers scarce pierce vacuums
left by your leaving, simply confirming
another year passed, an unkind kind of
commendation at coming through. Again.
Aware, in our footsteps, of things we said,
I feel you attached to my arm, hear me
pointing out how, head down, you miss
so much: the fields, ruins, nests in hedges,
cloudshapes, oh so often our fabled skies.
Now, eyes down for potholes and puddles,
sidestepping slow slugs and tripwire briars,
with my hands like claws and alien veins,
I may be becoming you, so tell, is this
the way of endings? Preoccupied with
things earthbound, ground level, before
heads tilt and eyes can turn to heavens?

II Harvest, Night Marsh Lane

Heavy with thistledown and harvestfug,
air in the lane closes, wraps round, cloys;
tongue tastes it, nose smells dust and diesel,
ears hear engines and wrong place alarms

like a Securicor van backing thro' a precinct,
yet this is fieldville: banks sport teazels, trees,
night safe is getting through without predation.
Beyond a hedge swirled through by dustfog

a green behemoth, with satellite precision,
manoeuvring to plane and shave another line
of field. With it a tractor and trailer waiting
close on its bidding, willing as any lover,

to sidle close beside, move at the command,
await the phallic pipe's swing for the act to
begin, and quick it shoots its load, no pause,
preliminaries or build-up, before moving on

as they, bearing another's seed, adjust gear,
and head to barns or driers. Harvest is urgent,
needs amber lights flashing hints of autumn
through the tan mists threshed from summer.

At Gressenhall we watched horse-drawn
harvesters, fragile, temperamental and slow.
You recalled those clean, clear-air summers:
days above and beyond most others helping,

in your nine-year-old way, stooking sheaves;
and how they harvested from outside in,
until one square of crop stood at the centre
hiding a fieldsworth of rabbits, rats and mice

seeking sanctuary. Then at an adult's word,
the kids tore in, shrieking, to shock them out.
You, complicit with guns and easy promises
of rabbit pie and stew enow for a fortnight.

III Primroses

She lives on in Little Marsh Lane:
your mum (hatted, coated, corsetted)
properly dressed for spring, leaning
to prod a tangled deke with her stick,
defying grass and brambled twiggery,
seeking out hidden primrose clumps.
This currency she gave, passed down,
gathered with love, carried to her
kitchen table for sorting and tying
with wool for its tenderness to stems:
posies for family, given simply because
she could; her way was to love large.
Pulled from places she once picked
stones or strawberries for shillings
for food, long before flowers for free.

There was a gap in flowers I gave you,
from frail few violets, fistful primroses
culled from railway cutting playgrounds,
before be-ribboned bouquets, crackling
with cellophane. And then the final flowers.
With a March burning of bones it was
meet I revisited your lane, probing edges.
As official lilies were wired to wreathes
I wound wool round primrose heads: a large
yellow mushroomed posy, resting with you,
facing us as we processed, chauffeured,
limousined, dark like gentry. Surely this was
our moment, your spirit radiant in farewell,
not the cold cheek kissed in a pillared room
where music drifted from hidden speakers.

(Note – *deke:* roadside bank.
Dialect, North Norfolk)

YOU READ TO ME STILL

You read to me still, your voice sounding
as new and fresh as in fond recollection:
of nights and stories we shared as though
we practised staying awake and telling for
long, loved, shared-bed evenings cajoling
sons with tales, down the earlobe caressed,
toasty and teddy'd, cottoned slopes to sleep.

And you, as parents begin to dim and fade
for love and need of something kind to do
(when, with endings, nothing can be done)
read quaint books your mother gifted you –
words spill on sheets, drift deep at cot sides;
unsure any are heard or pierce the emptiness,
grateful for faint smiles, the flicker of an eye.

And still you come, your patience familiar,
always animating voices the classroom way,
never faltering when eyelids close too long
to appreciate the pictures you conjure on air.
I am lost among your words, cosy as a child,
until another chapter winds toward its close
and a rare communion, too late exalted, ends.

AFTERWORD & ACKNOWLEDGEMENTS

Opportunities to acknowledge those people who have contributed, at key times and in varied ways, to a life shared with poetry and writing are rare and I would like to highlight a few individuals here. Some are no longer with us, but their input, influence and encouragement has endured and helped give shape and added purpose to years spread across more than half a century.

Early on at the Norfolk College of Arts and Technology, James (Jim) Sharpe helped kick-start the process by encouraging expression through creative writing; then John Coombes and Chris Emberson became inspirational guides on journeys of discovery through texts set by exam boards.

While studying for A levels there, Percy Greenfield, a respected editor of the *Lynn News & Advertiser,* bought and published my first feature article and went on to offer employment as a trainee reporter. Later, in the 1980s, Martin Throssell, assistant editor on the *Eastern Daily Press,* then a fine broadsheet, allocated space for leader page essays.

With pleasure and gratitude I remember a quartet of Yorkshiremen who presented opportunities in the early 1970s which provided a good foundation to build on. They are: George Cairncross, guiding spirit of the Fiasco Publications empire; the late Steve Sneyd of *Ludd's Mill* magazine; the late Alfred Bradley, former Head of Drama, BBC Northern Region, and founding producer of Radio 3's showcase of new writing, *The Northern Drift;* and poet Clifford Nicholas, then exiled in West Norfolk.

The late Ruth, Lady Fermoy, showed massive faith in an awkward, long-haired seventeen-year-old, allowing space to stage poetry and music programmes as part of King's Lynn Festival of Music and the Arts and later accepted an invitation to become Patron of Centre Poets. In the 1980s Cecilia Garnett, managing director at Hereward Radio, offered airtime on independent local radio to co-present spoken word programmes.

A special debt is owed to another son of Yorkshire, the late Howard Sergeant MBE of Outposts Publications for his support and confidence. Later, Anne Lewis Smith of *Envoi* magazine in West Wales and, more recently, Colin Blundell at Hub Editions, just across the county border in Lincolnshire, provided expert help and wise counsel as editors and publishers.

I was fortunate to enjoy the encouragement and friendship of poet, the late Edward Storey, as we ploughed literary furrows in our separate parts of the Fens and particularly after becoming part of Eastern Arts' Writers In The Community project enthusiastically managed by Irene Macdonald, the organisation's Literature Officer.

In a collection containing several poems evoking travel, it seems appropriate to acknowledge the team at Troubador Publishing who have been alongside as *Towards Babingley* took shape, especially Hannah Dakin, Joshua Howey de Rijk, Meera Vithlani, Lauren Stenning and designer Chelsea Taylor. I couldn't have wished for more expert guides on the journey towards publication.

I'm also grateful to Sue Burge and Janet Blundell for leading writing workshops where some poems among these pages had their beginnings, and to Colin Blundell again who, while editor of the British Haiku Society's journal, *Blithe Spirit,* led a day where he shared his inspirational enthusiasm for the form.

Teachers, editors, magazines, publishers and patrons come and go but, since 1981, one person has been constant with her support and committed belief in my writing. Mere thanks and words of appreciation seem barely adequate when many of the poems might not have life without her but, nevertheless, Tina, thank you – immeasurably, for everything.

HISTORICAL NOTE

The area around Babingley, which inspired a number of poems in this collection, is situated between Castle Rising, North Wootton and Wolferton, bordering the Wash in West Norfolk. The village currently consists of a once moated Hall and the base and broken shaft of a medieval stone boundary cross. A few cottages, social club and a mission church, a so-called tin tabernacle, dating from 1880 and home to a British Orthodox congregation, complete the former civil parish which was abolished and merged with Sandringham in 1935.

Felix of Burgundy (later Felix of Dunwich, subsequently canonised) is believed to have landed at Babingley, then a settlement alongside the estuary, having been invited by King Sigeberht of East Anglia to evangelise his Anglo-Saxon kingdom. In the *Ecclesiastical History of the English People,* well-known Jarrer-lad, go-to Geordie historian and fellow monk, the Venerable Bede, wrote that Felix saved "all the province of East Anglia from long-standing unrighteousness and unhappiness".

The ruined fourteenth-century church dedicated to Saint Felix, surrounded by fields to the west of the current hamlet, is believed to have been built on the site of the first Christian church to be built in Norfolk. By the nineteenth century the church ceased to be used and worship transferred to the smaller mission church.

The ruin, with an imposing tower rising over reclaimed marshlands, stands on private land and there is no public access. Viewed across fields from Old Hunstanton Road, Castle Rising, it is possible to see the nave, infilled chancel arch and the east window's outline. The structure has no roof. A south-facing porch, believed to have been added in Tudor times, is similarly dilapidated.

One and a quarter miles away, as the red kite soars, north-west of the ruins and bordering the former estuarine inlet, stands

Wood Farm at Wolferton. The farmhouse was formerly home to Prince John, youngest of six children born to King George V and Queen Mary, who died there in 1919 aged 13 years. More recently it became the private country retreat of the late Queen Elizabeth II and the Duke of Edinburgh.

The much diverted River Babingley, a clear Norfolk chalk stream, rises east of Flitcham and eventually finds its way across Wootton Marshes, then via the River Ouse into the Wash, passing close to the ruined church, and the supposed site of the original Saxon church. The river once powered a number of watermills including, close to Castle Rising and south of West Newton, mills producing paper and grinding corn. Both sites are now converted to residential use.